BLS WORKING PAPERS

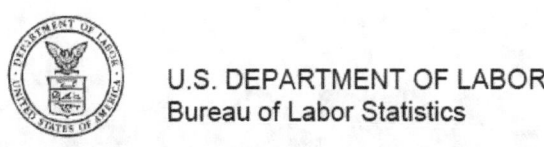 U.S. DEPARTMENT OF LABOR
Bureau of Labor Statistics

OFFICE OF PRICES AND LIVING
CONDITIONS

Explaining Tranquility in the Midst of Turbulence:
U.S. Multinationals' Intrafirm Trade, 1966-1997

Subramanian Rangan, INSEAD

Working Paper 336
January 2001

The views expressed are those of the author and do not necessarily reflect the policies of the U.S. Bureau of Labor Statistics or the views of other staff members.   This paper was part of the U.S. Bureau of Labor Statistics Conference on *Issues in Measuring Price Change and Consumption* in Washington, DC, June 2000.

Explaining Tranquility in the Midst of Turbulence:
U.S. Multinationals' Intrafirm Trade, 1966-1997

Subramanian Rangan
INSEAD
Bd de Constance
Fontainebleau
France 77305

Email: subramanian.rangan@insead.fr
Tel: 33-1-60.72.43.14

(Paper prepared for the Bureau of Labor Statistics June 5, 2000 conference)

I thank Bill Alterman, Catherine Mann, Illian Mihov, Paolo Fulghieri, Robert Lawrence, Raymond Mataloni, Jeffrey Reuer, Lorraine Eden, Christoph Loch, William Zeile, and Matthew Krepps for helpful comments.

U.S. international (export and import) prices enter into the calculations of the U.S. GDP deflator and the U.S. inflation index. Over the past couple of decades, as the international sector of the U.S. economy has shot up in relative importance, concern for the correctness of those international prices has grown too (see Alterman, 1997). Correct measurement of international prices is, however, a challenging task made more complicated by multinational firms' intrafirm transfer pricing. Considerable research has been devoted to understanding multinational transfer pricing (see Eden, 2000). By comparison, however, relatively little has gone into understanding the very driver of the multinational transfer pricing issue, viz., multinational *intrafirm trade*. It is, hence, this latter topic that I want to take up in this paper.

In particular, focusing on one important portion of U.S. intrafirm trade, viz., U.S. manufacturing multinationals' intrafirm exports, I want to address three questions. First, over the past three or four decades, have U.S. manufacturing multinationals' intrafirm exports become more important or less important in total U.S. manufacturing exports? In other words, is the complication winding itself up or down? Even among informed observers, views on the question are split. Some, noting the staggering rise in foreign direct investment, a growing trend among U.S. firms to multinationalize, and the growth in intra-industry trade, speculate that over these last decades the relative share of intrafirm trade must have trended up (and perhaps even sharply so). Others, pointing to the tremendous pressures and opportunities for "outsourcing" that U.S. firms have experienced over this time period, argue that, even in international exchange, arm's length transactions must, on balance, have displaced internal ones. As a result, these latter observers speculate, the relative importance of intrafirm trade must have declined (and perhaps even sharply so). In reality, as I show below, over the thirty years spanning 1966-1997 (which includes the earliest and the latest year for which relevant data are currently available), the share of U.S. multinationals' intrafirm exports in total U.S. manufacturing exports has remained remarkably stable at around 28 percent (see also Zeile, 1997).

This brings me to the second question. Considering that the views sketched above are not unfounded, how, in the midst of the *multinationalization* and *marketization* turbulence implied in those views, can we explain the relative tranquility in the U.S. intrafirm export ratio? To put it more simply, what explains the observed pattern in U.S. intrafirm exports? Existing theory, an offshoot of transaction cost economics, highlights failures and inefficiencies in arm's length trade in intangibles (see the section on intrafirm trade in Casson, 1990; Caves, 1996). For the most part, though, that theory is oriented at the cross-sectional level (i.e., it aims to explain cross-industry variation in propensity to trade intrafirm), and it does not purport to explain patterns over time. In an attempt to do so, I draw upon both relevant micro-level developments (such as advances in information technology and the rise in import competition) and attendant shifts in strategies of U.S. multinationals, and advance some new hypotheses on the drivers of intrafirm trade.

I then explore those hypotheses with a dataset that I constructed for the purpose. To be clear upfront, I should note that the data are far from ideal. For instance, while the hypotheses are oriented at the level of the firm, the data are at the industry level. (Firm level data on most of the relevant variables are simply unavailable.) Further, the set of firms that underlie these data is mostly but not strictly fixed over the time period studied.

3

Likewise, in the case of certain industries that are dominated by a few large firms(e.g., tobacco), the relevant data are, for confidentiality reasons, suppressed. Those pieces of data are, hence, missing. Lastly, while the hypotheses developed below are meant to be applicable to intrafirm trade in general, the empirical analysis undertaken here is limited to only one portion, viz., *U.S. parents'* exports. I am unable to include intrafirm exports of *foreign parents* due to a lack of data on key independent variables relating to those foreign parents. I will nevertheless make some brief remarks about trends in their role in U.S. intrafirm exports. (Zeile, 1997, and Mataloni, 1999 provide excellent overviews of the recent data on the import side and on the U.S. operations of foreign parents.)

Despite the limitations mentioned above, it is interesting and, likely, instructive, to pursue the empirical exploration. As I explain below, for the purpose at hand, industry aggregation is not a serious drawback. (In fact, all previous empirical studies of intrafirm trade have been conducted at the industry level.) Importantly, previous studies have tended to be cross-sectional rather than longitudinal, and, certainly, none spans such a long time period as the 30-year period covered here. That, combined with the fact that previous studies have not considered the role of factors such as technology advances and import competition, makes it likely that the empirical analysis contemplated will shed new light and help improve our understanding of the phenomenon of multinational intrafirm trade.

On that assumption, I take up a third question: Looking to the future, what projections can we make about the relative magnitude of intrafirm trade in total U.S. trade? To anticipate, let me just say that the analysis below suggests that relative share of intrafirm trade is unlikely to decline in the near future. Indeed, the vigilance that the

Bureau of Labor Statistics is exhibiting on this issue is warranted, and, pending a resolution on questions regarding price measurement methodology, should be maintained.

To recap, focusing on U.S. manufacturing multinationals' exports, I will first establish how the share of intrafirm trade has moved over the 30 year period between 1966-1997. I will then attempt, with the aid of some new hypotheses and a novel dataset, to empirically explain those past movements. I will conclude with remarks about the likely future direction that this ratio will take, and offer some comments for the BLS international price index program.

Intrafirm Shares in U.S. Manufacturing Exports, 1966-97

Figure 1 contains two panels showing movements in U.S. *non-fuel* manufacturing exports between 1966 and 1997. (Note, in both panels, the x-axis runs 1966, 1977, 1982, 1983,…,1997. Also, henceforth, manufacturing refers to non-fuel manufacturing, and exports refers to manufacturing exports.) Returning to Figure 1, the panel on the left shows that between 1966 and 1997 U.S. manufacturing multinationals' (intrafirm and total) exports have more or less tracked total U.S. manufacturing exports.

The panel on the right in Figure 1 shows trends in three ratios. These ratios indicate the relative importance of U.S. multinationals and their intrafirm trade in U.S. manufacturing exports. Among the three, the key ratio for our purpose is the percentage share in total U.S. manufacturing exports that is accounted for by U.S. parent's intrafirm exports. This share is depicted by the dotted line that runs lowest in the right-hand panel. Its striking characteristic is the stability, between 25 and 30 percent, that it exhibits over such a long period. The actual (and industry-disaggregated) figures behind this pattern are presented in the first set of columns in Table 1.

As for the other two ratios plotted in the right-hand side panel in Figure 1, the solid line at the top depicts U.S. manufacturing multinationals' total share in U.S. manufacturing exports. Note, that share includes U.S. parents' arm's length exports as well. Glancing at Table 1, we can see that from its high of 70 percent in 1977, that total share has been declining steadily, and, in 1997, it stood at 57 percent. Finally, the dashed line in the middle of the right-hand side panel in Figure 1 depicts the intrafirm share in U.S. parents' total exports. As can be seen from the chart, and more clearly from the figures in Table 1, this share has been rising gradually over the last two decades and now stands at nearly 50 percent (49.6 to use the exact figure in Table 1).

It should be easy to see that the dotted line (i.e., intrafirm share in total U.S. trade) is simply the product of the solid line (i.e., multinational share in total U.S. trade) multiplied into the dashed line (i.e., intrafirm share in total multinational trade). We thus have at least a mechanical explanation for the relative flatness of U.S. parents' intrafirm share in total U.S. exports: the multinational share in total U.S. trade has been declining but the intrafirm share in multinational trade has been rising. The behavior of U.S. firms that participate in the economy's international sector has apparently been subject to some real but opposing influences. For that reason, those shifts don't stand out in a summary indicator such as intrafirm trade in total U.S. trade.

Before delving into those opposing influences, let me refer to Table 2, which contains some summary data on U.S. multinationals and their foreign operations. The figures in this table suggest that, measured in terms of the number of U.S. parents and

6

foreign affiliates, multinationalization has been growing. Also, as indicated by the foreign employment share in U.S. parents' total employment, the relative importance of their foreign operations has grown, rising from 21 percent in 1966 to 36 percent in 1997. As I will show below, this latter development has had a significant effect on U.S. intrafirm trade.

To round out the overall picture on U.S. manufacturing exports (and also give a glimpse of the role of foreign multinationals) I tabulate some other data in Table 3. There first notice that over the past twenty years as foreign multinationals have established manufacturing operations in the United States, their total and intrafirm exports as a share of U.S. exports have risen sharply (going from 3.8 and 1.5 percent respectively in 1977 to 11.4 and 5.9 percent in 1997). The trend is similar for foreign parents' U.S. affiliates that are engaged in wholesale trade. Thus, in 1997, one-sixth of U.S. exports were accounted for by the U. S. affiliates of foreign parents. If the intrafirm exports of these foreign parents are added to the intrafirm exports of U.S. parents, then, as shown in the last row of the table, the "total" intrafirm share in U.S. manufacturing exports has trended up from an estimated 32 percent in 1977 to 39 percent in 1997.

Over the same period, the share of U.S. exports accounted for by purely domestic enterprises has nearly doubled (rising from 12 to 22 percent). The relative displacement has been absorbed in U.S. parents' share in total U.S. exports. In round numbers, U.S. manufacturing and wholesale parents' shares in U.S. exports have declined from 70 and 11 percent respectively in 1977, to 57 and 5 percent in 1997. In total, therefore, there has been a displacement of nearly 20 percentage points.

Having reviewed these longitudinal patterns in U.S. multinational and intrafirm trade, I will now turn to explanations of those patterns. My primary focus will, of course, be on explaining intrafirm trade and its evolution.

Explaining Intrafirm Trade

In terms of theory, as noted at the outset, the existing literature has addressed itself mainly to cross-industry variations in intrafirm trade. In particular, that literature has emphasized two factors. First, research (or *R&D*) intensity has been advanced as a key explanator. The argument is that in research-intensive industries firms are less able to rely on arm's length markets. Those markets are not congenial for transacting intangible (research) inputs and outputs. On the other hand, the internal mode, though likely more costly, is better-suited to mitigating certain serious downside risks (e.g., the misappropriation of proprietary knowledge). Hence, firms in R&D intensive sectors are more likely to internalize their exchange transactions (see Caves, 1996).

This preceding transaction costs-industrial organization logic has been coupled with the trade aspect of international business to explain the propensity of firms to engage in intrafirm cross-border trade. With few exceptions (see, for example, Benvignati, 1990), the R&D-intensity perspective has found broad empirical support (see Iall, 1978; Buckley and Pearce, 1979; Helleiner and Lavergne, 1979; Sleuwagen, 1985; Kobrin, 1991).

A second factor that is mentioned in explanations of intrafirm trade is the role of plant-level scale economies. Where the benefits of plant-level scale economies outweigh costs of transport, firms are more likely to centralize operations and distribute intermediate or finished goods (see Brainard, 1997). In empirical studies, however, the scale variable has not always performed as expected (see Helleiner and Lavergne, 1979; Benvignati, 1990; Kobrin, 1991). Researchers have suggested that weak results on this variable reflect the difficulty in correctly measuring and operationalizing scale economies.[1]

Beyond the R&D and scale factors highlighted in the cross-section-focused literature, I want to advance two other sets of factors as potential explanators of the *evolution* of intrafirm trade. Consider first a variable that I will refer to as *multinational intensity*. In simple terms, this variable is a measure of the relative magnitude and depth of firms' foreign operations. Firms set up operations in a foreign country when the volume of anticipated sales in the local or regional market grows large enough to justify the extra costs involved. The establishment of foreign operations tends, *over time*, to have two important influences on trade.

One, as firms grow their foreign presence, i.e., as they increase their multinational intensity, they grow too their ability to penetrate local and regional market. The volume of business they conduct with existing foreign customers grows; they acquire new foreign customers; and, importantly, they become more likely to introduce second and subsequent product lines into the market. As a consequence, *other things equal, as multinational intensity rises, the share of multinational trade in total trade between home and abroad should tend to rise as well.*

Two, as firms deepen their operations abroad, it becomes optimal to source more inputs locally. Of course, not all inputs can be sourced locally. There will likely remain

---

[1] While R&D and scale factors have received most attention in the existing literature, certain other factors, such as advertising intensity and locational factors, have also been mentioned in the literature (see the

certain proprietary or scale-sensitive inputs that firms will want to continue to source non-locally (typically, from home). Trade in these inputs is, however, more likely to be conducted intrafirm than at arm's length. What is more, once an affiliate is established abroad, it may act as an "inducement to indulge in transfer-price manipulations" (Lall, 1978: 216), and trade between home and abroad is more likely to be channeled via the affiliate. For these reasons, *other things equal, as the intensity of foreign operations rises, parents' trade between home and abroad will tend to become more intrafirm.*[2]

Another relatively recent development that is likely to push up intrafirm trade shares is something I will refer to as *multinational horizontal specialization.* In horizontal specialization, multinational firms allocate worldwide or at least regional responsibility for the production of certain intermediates and finished products to operations in specific countries (see Yi, 2000). Thus product A might be made (for world supply) in country X, while product B might be made in country Z (again, for world supply). This manner of within-firm cross-geographic specialization is reported (at least anecdotally) to have risen in the last couple of decades. The trend is being driven, it is thought, by such factors as increasing competition (and the attendant pressures for greater efficiency), the rising impact of exchange rate changes (and the quest by firms for a structural hedge), and increasingly common regional content requirements. Regardless, *other things equal, an increase in multinational horizontal specialization is likely to be accompanied by an increase in the internalization of trade.* After all, the workability and

---

studies mentioned in Caves, 1996: 32-33).

[2] To be clear, although the preceding hypotheses have not received explicit attention or much empirical scrutiny in the commonly cited studies of intrafirm trade, they are not entirely novel either. In fact, referring to studies by Swedenborg (1979) and others, Caves (1996: 33) has written, "The heavy participation of foreign subsidiaries in trade the and the complementarity of interaffiliate trade with their local production (and sales) activities is well established."

net benefits of such a strategy must call for greater intrafirm coordination. The latter is more likely to be achieved when trade flows are intrafirm.

To recap, higher levels of multinational intensity should lead to both a higher share of intrafirm trade and a higher multinational share in total U.S. trade. Higher levels of horizontal specialization should lead to higher intrafirm share in multinational trade. The view that, over the last three decades, the levels of multinational intensity and horizontal specialization have trended up is not very controversial. (Data reviewed in Table 2 and some to be reviewed below support this view.) In fact, it is these sorts of trends that adherents of the "multinationalization" school focus on, and, on the basis of which they conjecture that intrafirm trade has trended up.

Adherents of the "marketization" school, meanwhile, focus on forces that push down the share of intrafirm trade. I will discuss two important forces that fall in this category. First and foremost is the technology of coordinating economic exchange. I will simply refer to this as *technology*. The argument is as follows: as the relative cost of conducting arm's length exchange declines, firms' relative reliance on arm's exchange should rise (see Lawrence, 1995). Equally, if not more importantly, as the relative benefits of coordinating across arm's length catch up with the benefits of internal coordination, firms' relative reliance on arm's exchange should rise. Accordingly, *other things equal, as the benefit-cost ratio of coordination-enabling technology rises, multinational intrafirm trade shares should decline.*

Further, advances in this technology should enable economic exchange that would otherwise call for either special organizational complements (such as those offered by the multinational form) or minimum size or both. In other words, as this technology advances, purely domestic firms should be able to and should engage more and more in international trade. Therefore, *other things equal, as the benefit-cost ratio of coordination-enabling technology rises, the multinational share in total U.S. trade should decline.* [3]

In reality there is some empirical and considerable anecdotal evidence (not only in the electronics and the computer industry, but also in apparel and the auto sector) that over these past decades firms are increasingly embracing vertical specialization and relying more on "outsourcing" (see, Lawrence, 1995; Magretta, 1998). Prime among the forces that go into explaining this trend is the advance of microprocessor (and the related communication, computing, and storage technologies that they drive). Accordingly, in the empirical exercise below, I will rely on crude estimates of trends over time in the benefit-cost ratio of computer microprocessors.

The second force highlighted by the "marketization" school is a rise in *competition.* As firms confront greater product (and financial) market competition, they tend to divest "non-core" businesses, rely more on outsourcing, and return to their "core competencies." Hence, for reasons similar to those discussed above, *other things equal, the greater the competition, the greater should be the role of arm's length trade and the lesser the role of intrafirm trade.*

---

[3] To illustrate the technology hypothesis, I will provide a simple hypothetical example. Induced by technology, a multinational firm spins-off some of its operations into a separate firm. The two firms, subsequently, maintain their export behavior. Imagine firm A used to export 10 units, 5 of them intrafirm. Assume the division it spun-off accounted for 3 of the exported units (all of which used to be exported intrafirm). After the spin-off, the two smaller units still export 7 and 3 units respectively. But the multinational now has an intrafirm ratio of only 2/7 (as opposed to 5/10). The smaller unit (which now, say, is not a multinational) continues to export 3 units. Under such a scenario, we would have more exporters, which is consistent with the facts. We would also see both a decline in the multinational share in U.S. exports, and a decline in the intrafirm share of multinational exports.

Empirical Analysis of Intrafirm Export Shares in U.S. Manufacturing, 1966-97

Dataset

To explore the preceding hypotheses, I constructed a panel dataset that included (i) estimates of the three multinational and intrafirm U.S. export ratios plotted in the right-hand panel in Figure 1, and (ii) indicators of the independent variables discussed above. Most of the data come from three sources: the U.S. Census Bureau, the U.S. Bureau of Economic Analysis, and the OECD. The data items and data sources are listed in Appendix 1.

In terms of coverage, the panel contains dependent and independent variables for the years 1966, 1977, 1982, 1987, 1992, and 1997. The years 1966 and 1997 are the earliest and latest years for which data on the dependent variable are available. Further, except for 1997, the other years are ones in which the BEA conducted *benchmark* (population-level) surveys of U.S. parents' foreign operations. Last, but not least, the fact that the years are spaced wide apart should help mitigate problems of serial autocorrelation.

Sector focus, as noted at the outset, is limited to manufacturing (which, as a sector, still dominates the U.S. trade picture). Within manufacturing, the data are disaggregated at the 2-digit SIC-level. That is the level of detail at which the BEA tabulates most of its data on U.S. multinationals and their foreign operations. The same reason (BEA detail of reporting) guides the choice of the seventeen two-digit industries included in the analysis.[4] Together, the six time periods—1966, 1977, 1982, 1989, 1994, 1997—and seventeen 2-digit industries give a maximum of 102 observations.

---

[4] The seventeen 2-digit industries covered are: food and beverages; chemicals and drugs; primary metals; fabricated metals; machinery; electrical and electronic equipment; motor vehicles; other transport (mainly

13

Each observation aggregates, for a given period and industry, relevant data for the subset of firms (all U.S. multinationals or all U.S. firms) that underlie that sector. It is, thus, possible (though, given the variables in question, not very probable) that such aggregation masks wide variations in the behavior of individual firms within a given sector. The ideal would be to obtain firm level data, but these are simply not publicly available (and that too for this long a time period). Fortunately, since there is no reason to believe that such masking systematically affects particular sectors or time periods, one should still be able to glean useful insights from the empirical exercise.

Variables

Table 4 lists and describes the dependent and independent variables. The primary dependent variable in the analysis is PIFUSX. This variable indicates U.S. manufacturing multinationals' intrafirm exports as a percentage of U.S. manufacturing exports. There are two secondary dependent variables. PXUSX indicates U.S. multinationals' total exports as a percentage of U.S. exports. PIFXPX indicates U.S. multinationals' intrafirm exports as a percentage of their own total exports.[5] Table 4 describes the independent variables so I will not repeat here.[6] That table also shows the bivariate correlations among the variables. At 0.97, the bivariate correlation between

---

aircraft); textile products and apparel; lumber, wood, and furniture; paper and allied products; printing and publishing; rubber products; miscellaneous plastics; glass products; stone, clay, and nonmetallic mineral products; and instruments and related products. Tobacco products, shown in Tables 1 and 2, is excluded in the analysis due to erratic data.

[5] Just to clarify, in these dependent variable labels, the P stands for U.S. parents (i.e., U.S. multinationals); IF stands for intrafirm; X stands for exports; US stands for United States. These capitalized letters are combined to indicate the ratio under consideration.

[6] Except I want to point out that it is in order to circumvent exchange rate and inflation issues that I use employee counts rather than (the more conventional) foreign assets or sales figures to measure the multinational intensity variable (PMNEINT).

TIME (a time trend) and the variable labeled TECH is the highest. Not surprisingly, TIME is also highly correlated with U.S. GDP and import competition.

Empirical Estimation

For the purposes of empirical estimation, I employ a fixed effects panel model. This choice is motivated by three reasons, all in keeping with the econometrics literature on panel data (see Hsiao, 1985; and Baltagi, 1995). First, the data cover the "population" (rather than a random sample) of U.S.-based manufacturing multinationals. Second, inferences are to be made only for that population. Third, there are certain relatively stable "effects" that vary across industry but that are not explicitly included in the model. These include the relative importance of transport costs, advertising intensity, and the feasibility of (or susceptibility to) outsourcing. Due to differences in the "modularity" of intermediates, outsourcing is more feasible in certain industries (such as autos and electronics) than in others (such as chemicals and metals). This modularity factor is hard to measure but likely important. Industry dummies should help pick up such effects. (In any case, simple OLS results are presented as well.)

I should also add that although the data span a thirty-year period, the stability in the subset of firms that drive the *values* of the variables is likely to be quite high. This is because that subset is composed of the large U.S. multinationals that have long populated the Fortune 500 lists. Also, because compliance with the BEA survey is mandated by the U.S. government, self-selection is not an issue. Accordingly, the empirical design is not subject to some of the classic limitations associated with panel data (see Baltagi, 1995: 6-7).

The equations to be estimated are variants of the following:[7]

$$\text{Intrafirm Share in U.S. Exports}_{it} = \alpha_i + \beta * \text{R \& D/Sales}_{it} + \gamma * \text{Multinational Intensity}_{it}$$
$$+ \delta * \text{Multinational Horizontal Specialization}_{it} + \varepsilon * \text{Import Competition}_{it}$$
$$+ \zeta * \text{Technology}_{it} + \eta * \text{Scale}_{it} + \theta * \text{Time}_t + \iota_{it}.$$

Results

Consider first the results shown in Table 5. The dependent variable there is PIFUSX, i.e., U.S. parent's intrafirm exports as percent of total U.S. exports. As column 1 shows, two of the key variables of interest, PMNEINT, i.e., multinational intensity, and TECH, i.e., advances in coordination-enabling technology, both perform as hypothesized. The coefficient on the former is positive and exhibits the highest *t*-stat, and the coefficient on the latter is negative and takes the second highest *t*-stat. On the other hand, the third variable of interest, IMPCOMP (the competition variable), is statistically significant but takes a positive and not, as hypothesized, a negative sign.

Before discussing that puzzling but interesting result, I want to briefly review the other two models in Table 5. The model in column 2 includes TIME (in place of TECH) and its results are virtually unchanged from those in column 1. Given the near perfect correlation between TIME and TECH, that finding is not surprising. The results presented in column 3 are the simple OLS results. There too, the signs and significance of the key variables remain unchanged.

As for the other variables, R&D/Sales does not take significance in the first two models in this table, but does so in the third model, which does not include the industry

---

[7] Readers wondering why regular trade variables such as income and exchange rates are not included are

16

dummies. That would suggest that the latter are picking up the R&D factor. The SCALE variable perform as expected in the first two models, but not in the simple OLS model. There is not much to say about the industry dummies except to note that the ones that took statistically significant coefficients do appear to be the advertising or modularity intensive industries such as chemicals (which includes pharma and toiletries) , machinery, and autos.[8]

Let me now return to the competition variable IMPCOMP. Recall, greater competition, it was argued, would be associated with greater focus on core businesses and greater outsourcing (and arm's length trade). But, at least as far as these empirical results go, it appears that the first response is what dominates here and what leads to higher intrafirm trade. The explanation would go as follows. In response to competition, multinational parents divest non-core businesses and refocus on core businesses and operations. Now, parents' propensity to engage in intrafirm trade is likely to be higher in core than in non-core business. Accordingly, as competition rises (and as the core to non-core business ratio rises), the multinational intrafirm trade share rises too. If this is the chain of causation, then IMPCOMP should also take a positive and significant coefficient in the model where PIFXPX, intrafirm share in parents total exports, is the dependent variable. (I will turn to that dependent variable momentarily.)

But another logic might also help explain the positive relationship between the share of multinational intrafirm trade and IMPCOMP. Perhaps multinationals are better placed to survive the onslaught of import competition. Hence, an increase in import competition could lead to a larger share for intrafirm trade in total not (only) because of

---

reminded that the dependent variables are all share variables.

refocus on the core and an attendant rise in intrafirm shares, but because the multinational to non-multinational ratio rose. To the extent this is a part of the story, we would expect IMPCOMP to take a significant and positive sign in the model where PXUSX, multinational exports in total U.S. exports, is the dependent variable.

Before moving on to that model, let me summarize by saying that the results in table 5 strongly support the view that both the forces of multinationalization and the forces of marketization have been at work, and, as hypothesized, they influence intrafirm in expected but opposing directions. This, it would seem, is what explains the tranquility in the U.S. intrafirm export ratio that is observed even in the midst of the turbulence unleashed by the forces of technology and globalization. I will say more about this in the concluding discussion.

Turn now to Table 6, which presents the results of the regressions explaining PXUSX, U.S. multinationals' exports as a share of total U.S. exports.[9] The results in Table 6 are entirely consistent with those in Table 5. Again, as shown in column 1, multinational intensity (which has risen as more firms have multinationalized, and as firms have multinationalized more) pushes up, as hypothesized, the multinational share in total U.S. exports. TECH takes a negative and statistically significant coefficient. That is, coordination-enabling technology pushes down, as hypothesized, the multinational share in total U.S. exports. It is interesting to note that the coefficient on the TIME trend(shown in column 2), while positive, takes only borderline statistical significance.

---

[8] If data on advertising intensity were available for the industries and years covered, that variable could be entered separately.

[9] The independent variables used in the models in Table 6 are virtually the same as those in the previous table. MNEHSP, the horizontal specialization variable is not relevant here and is not used; and the R&D/Sales ratio is for all U.S. firms in an industry (and not just for U.S. multinationals as was the case in Table 5).

While one should not read too much into this, that result would appear to strengthen the TECH story.

Surprisingly, IMPCOMP does not take significance in any of the models in Table 6. That is, increases in the level of import competition do not lead to increases in the share of U.S. exports accounted for by U.S. multinationals. Thus, the survivor bias explanation is not supported in these data. Of course, this means that the import competition variable must work via PIFXPX, U.S. multinationals' intrafirm exports as a share of U.S. multinationals' total exports.

Table 7 shows the results of the models where PIFXPX is the dependent variable. And, indeed, IMPCOMP is positive and statistically significant here. Given that the other independent variables control for technology (or a time trend) and multinational intensity, this result is consistent with the hypothesis that multinational parents responded to import competition by cutting to core businesses. In turn, their propensity to trade intrafirm rises.

A second interesting finding in Table 7 is that TECH continues to be negative and significant. That is, TECH not only reduced multinationals' share in total U.S. trade, it also reduced the intrafirm share in multinationals' own trade. This lends further support to the marketization (or vertical specialization) view. Also, PMNEHSP, the horizontal specialization variable shows signs of life in this table (see column 3). In the raw data (not shown) it is clear that horizontal specialization (i.e., affiliate-affiliate trade) is trending up, and the results here give at least some support for the view that that development is pushing up, as one would expect, multinationals' propensity to internalize cross-border trade. Lastly, it is noteworthy that in this table the R&D variable takes

19

significance even in models that include the industry dummies. Perhaps this is not surprising, because the theoretical reasoning around R&D-intensity is really strongest for the dependent variable in this table (as compared to those in the two previous ones).[10]

Alternative Explanations

As with most empirical patterns, here too there are several possible alternative explanations and I want to address three in particular. The first one relates to the mix of industries over this thirty year period. Could it be that over the 1966-1997 period the composition of sub-industries in U.S. manufacturing exports has become less R&D intensive? The answer is no. First, R&D is a control variable in the models estimated above. Second, even at the level of the overall manufacturing sector, U.S. exports come more not less from R&D-intensive industries. The same is true for the intrafirm exports made by U.S. multinationals.

Another alternative explanation relates to country mix issues. Could it be that the reason TECH is significant is that it is highly correlated with TIME, which itself is significant and negative because it is correlated with a rise in the share of U.S. exports destined for developing countries? Due to factors such as political instability and smaller size of foreign markets, multinational trade with developing countries tends to be more likely to take place at arm's length. This country mix variable, however, cannot

---

[10] The results in Table 7 are also less exposed to a drawback in the dataset that relates to industry classification. The BEA provides multinational and affiliate trade data by industry of parent (and that is the classification used in the paper). The Census Bureau reports trade data by product. The extent of the overlap is no doubt high, but it is far from complete. In Table 7, since both the numerator and the denominator in the dependent variable come from the BEA, the industry classification problem is mitigated.

explain why multinationals' share in U.S. exports has declined. The technology story can explain that key pattern.[11]

A third alternative explanation for the tranquility in intrafirm trade shares is related to the role of inward foreign direct investment. The story is simply that the reason U.S. multinational share in U.S. exports have declined is not because of technology and such, but rather because foreign firms operating in the United States now account for a big portion of U.S. exports. While that is certainly true, this does not explain why IMPCOMP does not come out negative and significant in the models (in Table 6) where U.S. multinationals share is the dependent variable. It also does not explain why technology takes a negative sign in models (in Table 7) where intrafirm share in U.S. multinationals exports is the dependent variable. Lastly, as we saw in Table 3, the biggest jump in U.S. exporters comes from the "other U.S. entities" category (which excludes both U.S. and foreign multinationals).

Thus, these alternative explanations (nor the others that I have considered), can readily refute the hypotheses and interpretation offered above.

Discussion

If we abstract up a level, we can see what the preceding empirical results really suggest. Over the past two or three decades, three exogenous forces have been influencing the *scope* of U.S. multinationals. Shifts in the scope, in turn, get reflected in the relative share of trade that is conducted intrafirm. I will elaborate briefly.

There are three dimensions to the scope of the firm. *Vertical scope* refers to the extent of internalization of activities in a given business. As outsourcing rises and the

---

[11] Product by country data needed to empirically sort out this alternative explanation is not available.

firm engages in fewer activities, vertical scope declines. *Horizontal scope* refers to the number and diversity of businesses that the firm is engaged in. As the tendency rises to divest non-core businesses and refocus on core businesses, firms' horizontal scope declines. *Geographic scope* refers to number and diversity of countries that firms operate in. As more firms expand to more countries abroad, their geographic scope rises.

Advances in coordination-enabling technology have led U.S. multinationals to decrease their vertical scope and outsource more. In turn, their need and propensity to internalize trade has declined. Hence, increases in TECH were associated with decreases in multinational and intrafirm trade. On the other hand, the increase in competition has led U.S. multinationals to decrease their horizontal scope and refocus on core businesses. In turn, U.S. multinationals' propensity to internalize trade has increased. Hence, increases in IMPCOMP were associated with increases (rather than decreases in) intrafirm trade. Lastly, liberalization and economic growth abroad have led U.S. multinationals to increase their geographic scope and expand abroad. In turn, their overall share of U.S. international trade has risen and their opportunity and propensity to internalize international trade has risen. Hence, increases in MNEINT were associated with increases in multinational and intrafirm trade.

The influence of the preceding contemporaneous developments have, at least at the level of the overall manufacturing sector, been roughly equal and opposing. It is as a result that the share of intrafirm trade in total U.S. trade has appeared relatively stable over the past three decades.

Taking stylistic liberty, I depict in Figure 2 the above described pattern of evolution in the scope of U.S. multinational firms. As can be seen in that figure, the emerging pattern resembles a "cone." To be clear, real confirmation of such a pattern will have to await further empirical work (preferably with firm-level data). Still, the considerable anecdotal evidence that is available is not at odds with the spirit of Figure 2.

Conclusion

Reminding readers that this study has only scratched the empirical surface of the intrafirm trade issue, let me turn to the question: Looking forward, what are the likely prospects for intrafirm trade? To address this question, I would like to refer back to the "exogenous" drivers. I will discuss technology first, and then globalization and competition.

Clearly, in the wake of the internet and the virtual industrial marketplaces being established on its back, one must believe that firms are likely to further reduce their vertical scope in the foreseeable future. After all, the technology of the internet could make the benefits of arm's length coordination rise even as its costs fall. Again, anecdotal evidence indicates that outsourcing is likely to be intensified in the internet economy.[12] A point that is implicit here is that as arm's length trade grows more and better coordinated, the operational and managerial distinction between "arm's length" and "intrafirm" is likely to diminish. One would have to refer to "strictly" arm's length trade versus the regular kind where information and interests between buyer and seller are somewhat aligned. All in all, the internet could pick up where the microprocessor left off and it could continue to power the TECH variable and its effects on intrafirm trade.

---

[12] CISCO, the famous router manufacturer, apparently has 35 factories making its products, of which it owns only four.

On the other hand, there are a set of equally important (but slightly more complicated) reasons why intrafirm trade could trend up. First, foreign parents are multinationalizing with unprecedented enthusiasm and many of them are entering the United States. This increase in the number of foreign multinationals with affiliates in the United States is likely to push up U.S. intrafirm trade. We saw indirect evidence for this in Table 1. But consider Figure 3, which plots intrafirm trade intensity against foreign presence intensity. The relationship is striking. If a firm has an affiliate in country A, then chances are high that its trade with country A will be internalized. (The benefits for doing so are many and some of them lead to the doorstep of the transfer pricing issue.)

The preceding pattern must explain why research-intensive firms do any arm's length trade at all. Their arm's length trade must be concentrated with countries where they do not yet have affiliates. The intrafirm trade ratios in foreign affiliate-U.S. parent shown in Table 8 lend strong support to this hypothesis. Looking down the last column of that table one would hardly be able to distinguish between high and low R&D industries. Essentially, when a parent has an affiliate abroad and that affiliate trades with the parent's home country, then the trade gets internalized.

But what drives the likelihood of establishing a foreign affiliate? The size of the local, national, or regional market. And therein lies the second point. As foreign markets grow, U.S. parents will be more likely to establish affiliates abroad. As that happens, U.S. parents' intrafirm trade propensity is going to rise. Accordingly, the establishment of U.S. affiliates by foreign parents and of foreign affiliates by U.S. parents is going to keep powering PMNEINT, which, in turn, is going to keep pushing up intrafirm trade shares.

24

The upshot is that technology and multinationalization are again likely to be pushing intrafirm trade shares in opposite directions. Another way to guess the likely direction of intrafirm share in total U.S. exports is look at the two underlying patterns: multinational share in total and the intrafirm share in multinational trade. As we saw above, the share of MNE trade in total U.S. trade has been trending down. If that trend accelerates, then even if intrafirm share in MNE trade rises, the net figure may go down. Yet, multinationals simply cannot be counted out. Rising trade, especially in manufactures of a high-tech or high-touch nature leads to multinationalization. Likewise, inward foreign direct investment often provokes outward foreign direct investment; and so on. What is more, the share of intrafirm trade in multinationals' total trade has, despite improvements in technology (and reduced transactions costs), been trending up. Increased multinationalization, increased horizontal specialization, and a return to core competencies all appear to have "caused" this outcome.

Accordingly, if the decline in multinationals' total share of U.S. trade reverses itself (a probable but not certain development) , we could see intrafirm shares in total U.S. trade rising (and perhaps sharply). But, over the near future (say over the next five years), one cannot rule out (and one must rule in) the continuation of the pattern of the last thirty years.

Implications for the BLS International Price Index

Based on this paper's data and analysis, I have three brief comments for the BLS International Price program:

(i) The special attention that the department has paid to the intrafirm trade and transfer pricing issue is warranted and should be maintained. While the share of intrafirm trade has declined in a few industries, it has, in general, not subsided over the past three decades. In fact, if the U.S. operations of foreign multinationals are taken into account, the share of intrafirm trade has grown. The pattern not only appears set to continue into the future, it may even be that the share of intrafirm trade rises further. The transfer pricing complication is, in other words, not about to wind itself down.

(ii) Since multinational firms themselves engage in both intrafirm and arm's length trade (and since the two sets of prices are often different in levels and changes in levels), it might be useful, even for deflation purposes, to collect and use the two sets of prices on two different sets of trade values. If only intrafirm or only arm's length prices are used to deflate all exports, then trade volumes might be incorrectly estimated. Of course, the burden on participating firms will be higher, and the Bureau will, no doubt have to come up with ways(such as internet reporting) to ease the burden.

(iii) Setting aside the question of legal and financial feasibility, I would suggest surveying final customers, at least in selected foreign markets. Even if done on a narrow basis, this could be valuable not only as a check on what is reported domestically, but also from the point of view of researchers that use the international price index for studies relating to U.S. firm's foreign pricing practices.

Appendix 1

Data Sources

Item	_Data Source_
U.S. manufacturing exports	U.S. Bureau of the Census, _Statistical Abstract of the United States_, various issues.
U.S. parents' intrafirm exports	U.S. Bureau of Economic Analysis, _United States Direct Investment Abroad_, various issues.
U.S. parents' total exports	U.S. Bureau of Economic Analysis, _United States Direct Investment Abroad_, various issues.
U.S. industry R&D as a percentage of current output	OECD, _Research and Development in Industry_, various issues. Also (for 1966) _Statistical Abstract of the United States: 1971_; and (for 1997) National Science Foundation/ Division of Science Resource Studies, _Survey of Industrial Research: 1997_.
U.S. parents' R&D as a percentage of sales	U.S. Bureau of Economic Analysis, _United States Direct Investment Abroad_, various issues.
U.S. parents' foreign and total employment	U.S. Bureau of Economic Analysis, _United States Direct Investment Abroad_, various issues.
Affiliate-to-affiliate trade share in U.S. majority-owned foreign affiliates' sales	U.S. Bureau of Economic Analysis, _United States Direct Investment Abroad_, various issues.
Imports, exports, and production in U.S. industry	OECD, _The OECD STAN Database for Industrial Analysis_, various issues.
GDP in U.S. industry (in constant dollars)	OECD, _The OECD STAN Database for Industrial Analysis_, various issues. Also (for 1966) _Statistical Abstract of the United States: 1971_; and U.S. BEA/ Industry Economics Division, _1947-1997, GDP in current dollars_.
Computing power (millions of instructions per second) per dollar	Estimated from Decision Resources, Inc., _Spectrum_. Frederic G. Withington, "The resurgence of the mainframe computer," March, 1997, 93: 1-11.
Plant scale (employees per establishment) in U.S. industry	U.S. Bureau of the Census, _Statistical Abstract of the United States_, various issues. Also, (for 1992) _Census of Manufactures: 1992_; and (for 1997) _Economic Census, 1997_.

References

Alterman, Bill, 1997. "Are producer prices good proxies for export prices?" *Monthly Labor Review*, October, pp. 18-32.

Baltagi, Badi H., 1995. *Econometric analysis of panel data*, New York: John Wiley & Sons.

Benvignati, Anita, 1990. "Industry determinants and 'differences' in U.S. intrafirm and arms-length exports." *The Review of Economics and Statistics*, August (3): 481-488.

Brainard, S. Lael, 1997. "An empirical assessment of the proximity-concentration trade-off between multinational sales and trade." *The American Economic Review*, **87**(4): 520-544.

Buckley, Peter J. and R. D. Pearce, 1979. "Overseas production and exporting by the world's largest enterprises: A study in sourcing policy." *Journal of International Business Studies*, **10** (Spring): 9-20.

Casson, Mark (ed.), 1990. *Multinational corporations*. Hants: Edward Elgar Publishing.

Caves, Richard E., 1996. *Multinational enterprises and economic analysis*, Cambridge: Cambridge University Press.

Eden, Lorraine, 2000. "International intrafirm trade, transfer pricing and the BLS international price program." Paper prepared for the Bureau of Labor Statistics, Washington, D.C., June.

Helleiner, Gerald K. and Real Lavergne, 1979. "Intra-firm trade and industrial exports to the United States." *Oxford Bulletin of Economics and Statistics*, **41** (November): 297-311.

Hsiao, Cheng, 1985. *Analysis of panel data.* Cambridge: Cambridge University Press.

Kobrin, Stephen, 1991. "An empirical analysis of the determinants of global integration." *Strategic Management Journal*, **12**: 17-31.

Lall, Sanjaya, 1978. "The pattern of intra-firm exports by U.S. multinationals." *Oxford Bulletin of Economics and Statistics*, **40** (August): 209-222.

Lawrence, Robert Z., 1995. *Single world, divided nations?* Washington, D.C.: Brookings Institution Press.

Magretta, Joan, 1998. "Fast, global, and entrepreneurial: Supply chain management, Hong Kong style. An interview with Victor Fung," *Harvard Business Review*, September-October: 103-114.

Mataloni, Raymond, Jr., 1999. "U.S. multinational companies: Operations in 1997." *Survey of Current Business*, **79** (July): 8-35.

Sleuwagen, L, 1985. "Monopolistic advantages and the international operations of firms: Disaggregated evidence from U.S.-based multinationals." *Journal of International Business Studies*, **16** (Fall): 125-133.

Swedenborg, Briggita, 1979. *The multinational operations of Swedish firms: An analysis of determinants and effects.* Stockholm: Industrial Institute for Economic and Social Research.

Yi, Kei-Mu, 2000. "Can vertical specialization explain the growth of world trade?" Federal Reserve Bank of New York, Staff Reports, No. 96, January.

Zeile, William, 1997. "U.S. intrafirm trade in goods." *Survey of Current Business*, **77**(February): 23-38.

Figure 1. Intrafirm and total share of U.S. multinational parents' exports in total U.S. non-coal, non-petroleum exports, 1966-97
(X-axis scale--the time line--is not continuous)

Index of the nominal value of U.S. exports
(1966 = 100)

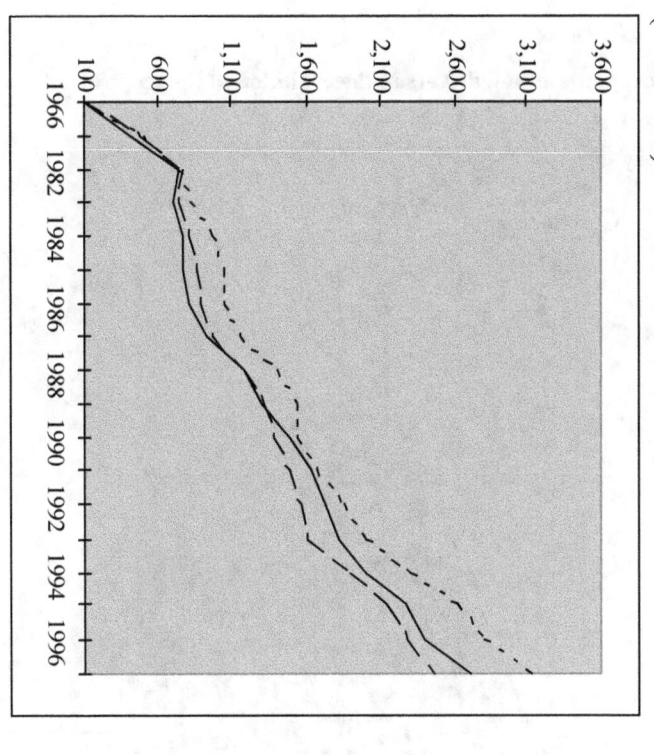

- - - Intrafirm exports of U.S. parents in manufacturing
- – Total exports of U.S. parents in manufacturing
——— Total U.S. (non-fuel) manufacturing exports

U.S. parents' intrafirm exports
(1966 = 100)

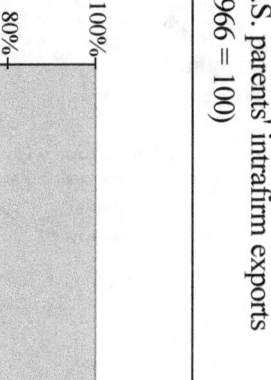
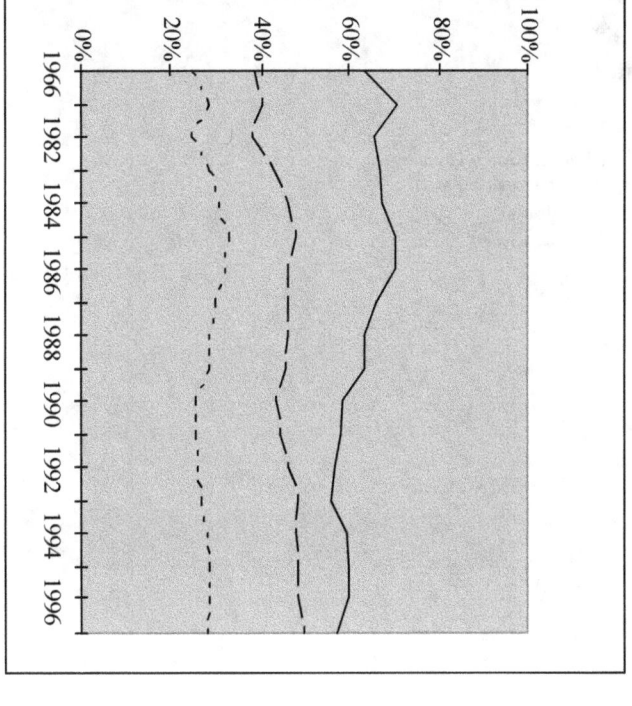

- - - Intrafirm share in total U.S. (non-fuel) manufacturing exports
- – Intrafirm share in manufacturing parents' total U.S. exports
——— Manufacturing parents' total share in U.S. (non-fuel) manufacturing exports

Source: U.S. Department of Commerce, *Statistical Abstract of the United States*, various issues; *U.S. Direct Investment Abroad*, various issues.

Figure 2. Gross patterns and drivers in the evolution of the scope of U.S. multinational firms

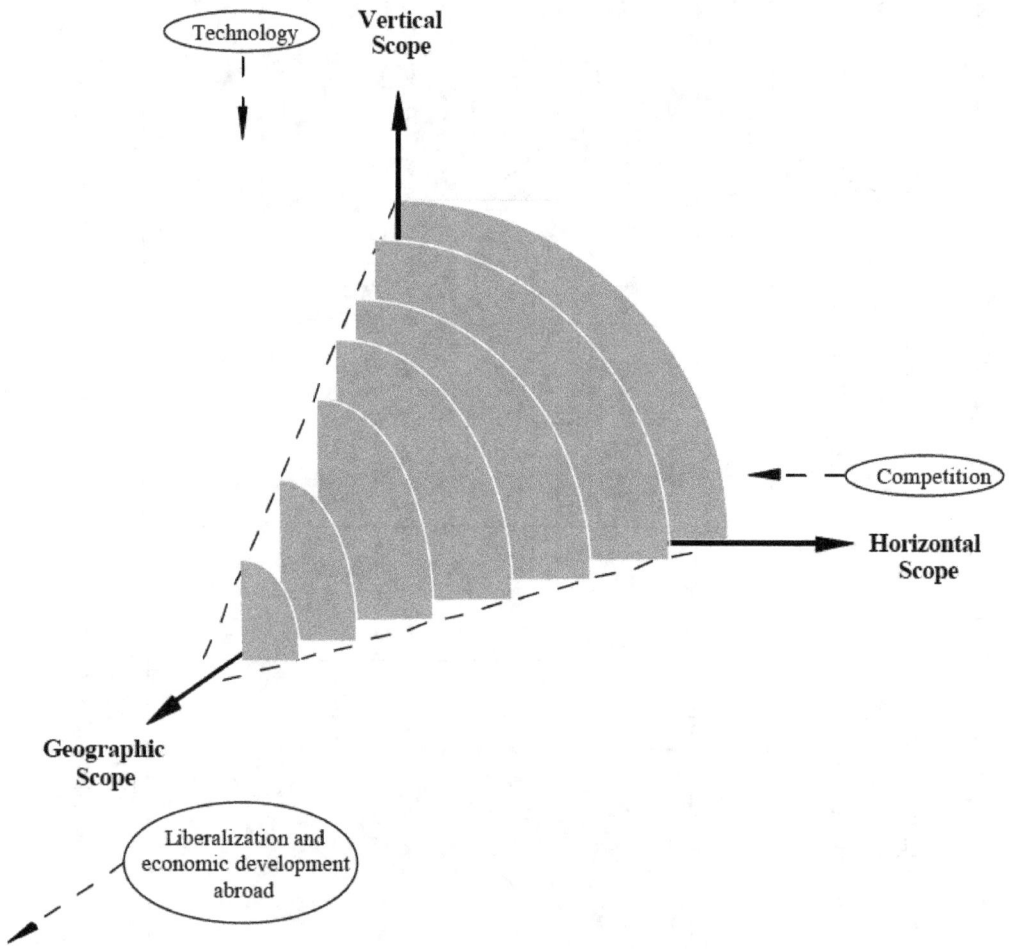

Figure 3. U.S. parents' foreign presence and their share of goods exports that is intrafirm, selected countries, 1994.

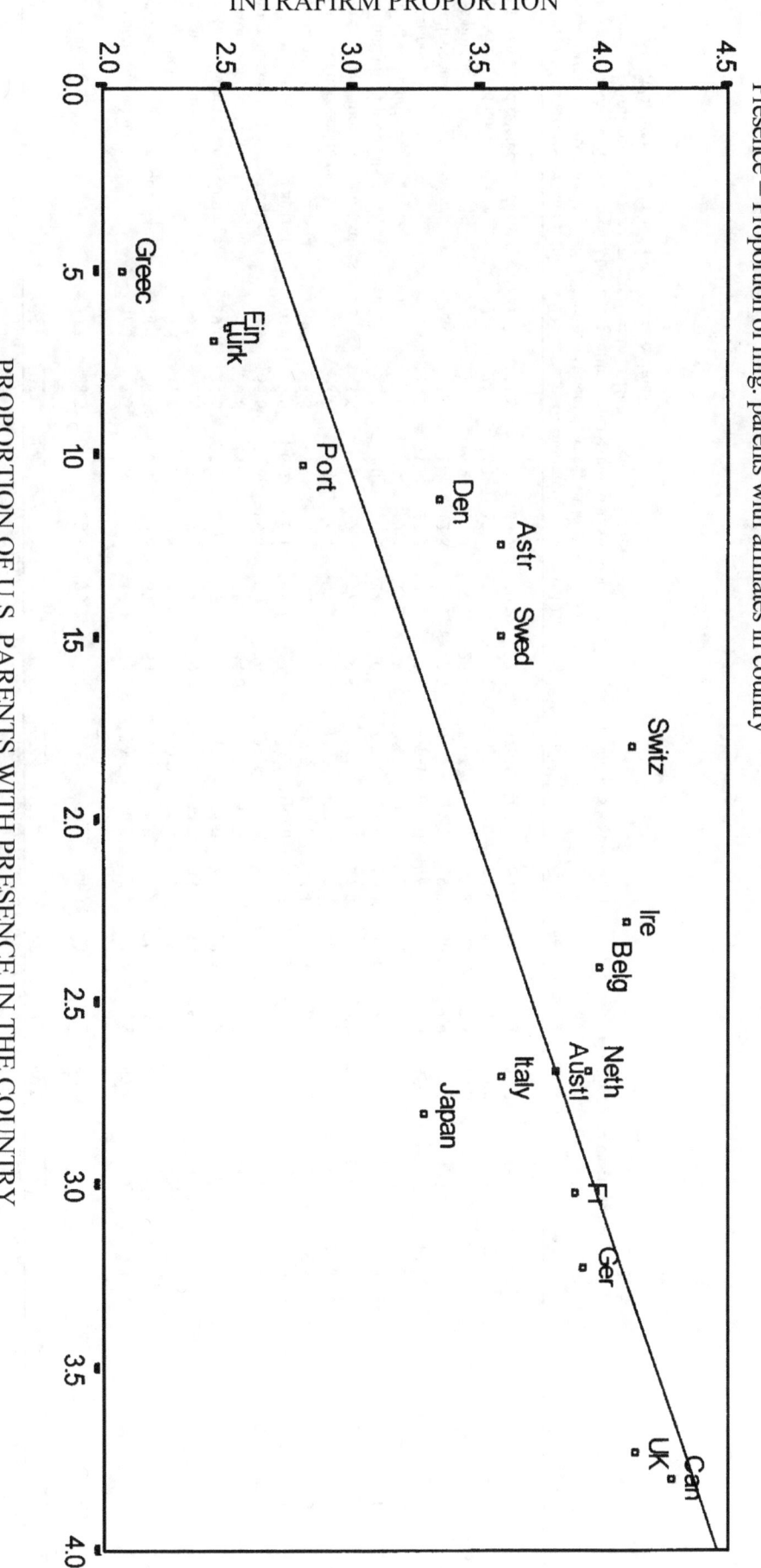

INTRAFIRM PROPORTION

Presence = Proportion of mfg. parents with affiliates in country

PROPORTION OF U.S. PARENTS WITH PRESENCE IN THE COUNTRY

Table 1. U.S. manufacturing parents' intrafirm and total exports as a percentage of U.S. manufacturing exports, 1966-97

Industry	U.S. manufacturing parents' intrafirm exports as a % of total U.S. manufacturing exports*						U.S. manufacturing parents' total exports as a % of total U.S. manufacturing exports*						U.S. manufacturing parents' intrafirm exports as a % of total U.S. manufacturing parents' exports					
	1966	1977	1982	1989	1994	1997	1966	1977	1982	1989	1994	1997	1966	1977	1982	1989	1994	1997
Manufacturing	24.5	28.5	24.7	28.8	28.2	28.4	62.8	70.4	64.9	63.0	59.2	57.2	39.0	40.5	38.1	45.6	47.6	49.6
Food and kindred products	7.3	7.3	6.8	9.9	16.3	18.8	24.5	36.9	35.1	64.8	84.8	67.6	29.9	19.7	19.5	15.3	19.2	27.8
Chemicals and allied products	28.5	38.4	30.4	34.6	37.0	34.1	69.0	85.9	80.2	70.8	72.6	60.9	41.3	44.7	37.8	48.8	50.9	56.0
Primary metals products	6.8	21.8	11.3	9.8	6.9	4.5	50.9	95.4	79.8	38.1	34.7	22.2	13.3	22.8	14.2	25.6	19.9	20.1
Fabricated metal products	37.3	9.6	8.7	8.3	9.5	9.3	99.0	33.0	35.9	35.5	25.3	31.4	37.7	29.1	24.1	23.4	37.3	29.6
Industrial machinery and equipment	19.6	24.6	25.3	41.3	37.4	34.6	58.0	58.0	49.8	58.4	57.8	53.3	40.0	42.3	50.9	70.7	64.7	64.8
Electronic and other electric equipment	23.1	29.8	28.7	23.0	24.5	34.0	70.4	87.3	89.5	63.2	56.5	70.0	32.8	34.1	32.1	36.4	43.3	48.6
Motor vehicles and equipment	68.5	66.6	71.6	89.4	70.9	76.7	127.5	92.1	94.9	113.3	91.2	99.3	53.7	72.3	75.5	78.9	77.7	77.3
Other transport (including aircraft)	10.4	9.0	6.3	6.1	5.9	4.3	60.5	130.0	96.7	85.5	82.7	80.2	17.2	6.9	6.5	7.1	7.1	5.3
Tobacco products	17.4	33.8	15.9	4.6	n/a	n/a	148.2	173.2	164.1	45.6	n/a	n/a	11.7	19.5	9.7	10.2	n/a	n/a
Textile products and apparel	4.1	8.0	3.8	4.9	3.4	2.0	13.9	27.7	18.8	16.7	11.5	10.9	29.4	28.8	20.0	29.3	29.6	18.4
Lumber, wood, furniture, and fixtures	3.2	3.6	2.8	2.5	7.0	9.5	8.7	44.6	41.0	48.1	23.7	27.0	36.8	8.0	6.9	5.2	29.7	35.0
Paper and allied products	22.7	22.4	7.0	10.5	24.2	20.6	73.7	57.9	50.5	61.1	87.8	73.0	30.8	38.7	13.8	17.2	27.6	28.2
Printing and publishing	11.3	18.0	9.4	9.4	7.2	7.3	35.3	41.2	28.0	20.6	17.1	19.3	32.0	43.8	33.4	45.4	42.4	37.9
Rubber products	n/a	46.3	34.5	23.7	26.1	22.1	n/a	115.0	76.3	47.8	57.5	35.7	49.0	40.3	45.2	49.6	45.4	61.7
Miscellaneous plastics products	20.8	5.7	2.7	12.8	5.9	3.3	55.5	19.2	9.3	30.8	22.9	12.7	37.6	29.7	29.2	41.5	25.9	26.2
Glass products	20.4	13.7	16.2	12.8	7.9	26.1	50.7	56.4	50.2	55.8	53.3	73.3	40.1	24.2	32.3	23.0	14.9	35.6
Stone, clay, and nonmetallic mineral	31.4	21.1	22.1	17.5	19.2	7.1	68.1	72.7	58.9	40.7	48.6	24.0	46.1	29.0	37.6	43.1	39.5	29.6
Instruments and related products	31.3	43.8	43.3	34.7	30.2	22.4	81.6	67.8	65.6	68.8	50.4	40.2	38.3	64.6	66.0	50.5	59.9	55.7

Source: U.S. export figures are from U.S. Department of Commerce, Statistical Abstract of the United States, various issues; multinational export figures are from U.S. Department of Commerce, U.S. Direct Investment Abroad, various issues.

*The U.S. Commerce Department classifies multinational export data by industry of U.S. parent and U.S. export figures by product. This, in some cases, leads to estimates of intrafirm shares that are greater than 100 percent of the total.

n/a not available; figures in italics are author's estimates.

Table 2. Number of U.S. parents and their foreign affiliates, and foreign employment of U.S. parents in manufacturing, 1966-97

Industry	Number of U.S. parents*				Number of foreign affiliates*				Foreign employment (in 000s)				Foreign employment in parents' total employment			
	1966	*1977*	*1989*	*1997*	*1966*	*1977*	*1989*	*1997*	*1966*	*1977*	*1989*	*1997*	*1966*	*1977*	*1989*	*1997*
Manufacturing	936	1,289	1,312	1,501	n/a	####	####	####	2,988	5,323	4,490	4,929	21%	31%	31%	36%
Food and kindred products	61	78	63	69	n/a	1,252	1,083	1,097	264	484	496	601	20%	32%	30%	45%
Chemicals and allied products	121	136	173	205	n/a	2,447	3,065	3,330	394	747	724	770	34%	38%	37%	44%
Primary metals products	n/a	53	55	65	n/a	552	364	323	92	285	129	117	8%	22%	27%	29%
Fabricated metal products	n/a	141	108	123	n/a	529	478	654	178	173	95	158	29%	26%	22%	33%
Industrial machinery and equipment	n/a	226	253	260	n/a	1,717	2,075	2,480	409	763	714	786	19%	28%	36%	42%
Electronic and other electric equipment	n/a	156	161	209	n/a	1,089	1,298	1,663	472	659	465	639	27%	34%	30%	35%
Motor vehicles and equipment	46	33	50	52	n/a	475	518	802	496	844	776	725	29%	38%	43%	45%
Other transport (including aircraft)	n/a	25	31	27	n/a	327	499	467	39	239	208	189	4%	16%	16%	20%
Tobacco products	n/a	6	10	6	n/a	111	274	243	9	77	124	71	7%	44%	45%	63%
Textile products and apparel	n/a	63	52	53	n/a	385	177	176	85	157	56	68	11%	19%	15%	19%
Lumber, wood, furniture, and fixtures	n/a	35	26	35	n/a	108	115	193	69	55	44	85	23%	17%	17%	24%
Paper and allied products	n/a	38	40	54	n/a	272	392	541	104	164	162	210	23%	32%	30%	33%
Printing and publishing	n/a	46	44	51	n/a	209	233	281	21	47	50	47	8%	16%	12%	13%
Rubber products	n/a	19	14	20	n/a	211	126	148	97	233	107	85	34%	44%	45%	37%
Miscellaneous plastics products	n/a	26	41	54	n/a	115	243	230	22	16	43	34	27%	20%	29%	25%
Glass products	n/a	8	9	13	n/a	103	54	119	42	70	38	66	32%	39%	27%	38%
Stone, clay, and nonmetallic mineral produc	n/a	23	20	21	n/a	225	109	85	48	80	39	23	28%	40%	31%	25%
Instruments and related products	n/a	97	118	126	n/a	659	842	1,030	117	181	202	223	28%	30%	24%	30%

Source: U.S. Department of Commerce, *U.S. Direct Investment Abroad*, various issues.

*Figures for number of U.S. parents and foreign affiliates in 1966 and 1977 are author's estimates. Estimates are made from the available data and the assumption that 50 and 70% of the parents and affiliates would have met the $3 million cutoff that is in use starting in 1982. The cutoff prior to 1982 was $500,000.

n/a not available; figures in italics are estimates.

35

Table 3. Intrafirm shares in U.S. non-coal, non-petroleum manufacturing exports accounted for by U.S. and foreign multinational enterprises, 1966-97

Figures are in percent unless stated otherwise

	Year			
	1966	*1977*	*1989*	*1997*
Non-coal, non-petroleum U.S. manufacturing exports (in millions of current dollars)	22,088	93,544	272,260	589,208
Percentage shares				
Total	**100.0**	**100.0**	**100.0**	**100.0**
Shipped by U.S. parents in manufacturing	62.8	70.4	62.8	57.2
To their majority-owned foreign affiliates	24.5	27.5	29.0	28.2
Shipped by U.S. parents in wholesale trade	6.5	10.8	5.8	4.7
To their majority-owned foreign affiliates	0.9	0.7	0.6	1.0
Shipped by U.S. manufacturing affiliates of foreign parents	n/a	3.8	11.7	11.4
To their parents and affiliates	n/a	1.5	4.9	5.9
Shipped by U.S. wholesale trade affiliates of foreign parents	n/a	3.1	6.8	5.3
To their parents and affiliates	n/a	1.9	4.6	3.5
Shipped by other U.S. entities	n/a	11.9	12.8	21.3
*Total intrafirm share in non-coal, non-petroleum U.S. manufacturing exports**	*25.4*	*31.6*	*39.1*	*38.6*

Source: Author's estimates based on data from U.S. Department of Commerce, *Statistical Abstract of the United States* , various issues; *U.S. Direct Investment Abroad* , various issues; *Foreign Direct Investment in the U.S.*, various issues.
n/a = not available.
* The total intrafirm share figure for 1966 is an underestimate since it excludes foreign parents' exports; the true figure is likely to be slightly higher (around 27 or 28 percent). On the other hand, the total intrafirm share figures for 1989 and 1997 are likely to be overestimates. The latter double count some U.S. exports by U.S. parents that are themselves U.S. affiliates of foreign parents.

Table 4. Descriptive statistics and zero-order correlations for variables related to U.S. intrafirm exports in manufacturing, 1966-97

Variable name and description	Num. of obs.	Mean (s.d.)	2	3	4	5	6	7	8	9	10	11	12
1. PIFXUSX U.S. parents' intrafirm exports as a percentage of total U.S. exports	101	20.7 (17.8)	0.67	0.82	0.50	0.20	0.66	0.53	0.39	0.17	-0.05	0.39	-0.04
2. PXUSX U.S. parents' total exports as a percentage of total U.S. exports	101	55.6 (27.6)	1.00	0.21	0.47	0.50	0.46	0.17	0.09	-0.06	-0.17	0.64	-0.17
3. PIFXPX U.S. parents' intrafirm exports as a percentage of U.S. parents' total exports	102	35.6 (17.5)		1.00	0.45	0.03	0.56	0.60	0.41	0.31	0.07	0.04	0.07
4. PRDSALE U.S. parents' R&D as a percentage of sales	102	2.5 (2.2)			1.00	0.69	0.36	0.52	0.35	0.33	0.10	0.38	0.09
5. USRDSALE U.S. industry R&D as a percentage of current output	102	2.9 (3.9)				1.00	0.00	0.15	0.19	0.16	0.00	0.52	-0.00
6. PMNEINT U.S. parents' foreign employment as a percentage of their total employment	102	28.2 (9.6)					1.00	0.53	0.37	0.28	0.25	0.27	0.24
7. PMNEHISP Affiliate-affiliate trade share in U.S. majority-owned foreign affiliates' sales	102	12.1 (6.0)						1.00	0.66	0.46	0.35	0.12	0.36
8. IMPCOMP Imports as a percentage of apparent consumption in U.S. industry	102	10.1 (8.2)							1.00	0.49	0.56	0.18	0.57
9. OUTPUT Log of GDP in U.S. industry (in constant dollars)	102	5.1 (0.5)								1.00	0.57	0.00	0.61
10. TECH Computing power per dollar [inverse of log(price/millions of instructions per second)]	102	0.9 (0.0)									1.00	-0.14	0.97
11. SCALE Plant scale in U.S. industry [log((employees/establishment) [2]]	102	8.4 (1.3)										1.00	-0.15
12. TIME [1966 = 1, 1977 = 12, ..., 1997 = 32]	102	19.1 (10.6)											1.00

Table 5. Regressions explaining intrafirm shares in total U.S. manufacturing exports, 1966-97

Variable	(1)	(2)	(3)
Constant	-47.64 **	-58.28 **	9.41
	(-2.03)	(-2.45)	(0.74)
PRDSALE U.S. parents' R&D as a percentage of sales	0.59	0.43	1.38 **
	(0.78)	(0.57)	(2.18)
PMNEINT U.S. parents' foreign employment as a percentage of their total employment	0.63 ***	0.61 ***	0.92 ***
	(4.51)	(4.31)	(6.42)
PMNEHSP Affiliate-affiliate trade share in U.S. majority-owned foreign affiliates' sales	-0.07	-0.05	0.39
	(-0.28)	(-0.19)	(1.32)
IMPCOMP Imports as a percentage of apparent consumption in U.S. industry	0.54 **	0.51 **	0.51 **
	(2.60)	(2.43)	(2.37)
TECH Computing power per dollar [inverse of log(price/millions of instructions per second)]	-262.24 ***		-450.57 ***
	(-3.79)		(-4.45)
SCALE Plant scale in U.S. industry [log((employees/establishment) ^{2})]	7.00 **	6.47 **	1.25
	(2.59)	(2.37)	(1.21)
TIME		-0.33 ***	
		(-3.50)	
Industry dummies			
Chemicals	14.39 ***	15.28 ***	
	(2.86)	(3.03)	
Primary metal	-9.55	-8.74	
	(-1.57)	(-1.43)	
Fabricated metal	10.88 **	10.42 **	
	(2.65)	(2.50)	
Machinery	17.15 ***	17.53 ***	
	(2.95)	(2.96)	
Electrical	-1.54	0.07	
	(-0.22)	(0.10)	
Motor vehicles and equipment	32.99 ***	35.07 ***	
	(3.81)	(4.07)	
Other transport (mainly aircraft)	-10.58	-9.18	
	(-1.47)	(-1.24)	
Other industry dummies	n/s	n/s	
No. of observations	101	101	101
Adj. R^2	0.90	0.89	0.60
F-stat	39.70 ***	38.68 ***	25.99 ***
Durbin-Watson	2.08	2.10	0.76

n/s not shown but included in the model. ***, **, and * indicate significance at the 1%, 5%, and 10% levels respectively. The dependent variable is PIFXUSX U.S. parents' intrafirm exports as a percentage of total U.S. exports. Observations are from seventeen 2-digit manufacturing industries (excluding tobacco) and six time periods: 1966, 1977, 1982, 1994, 1989, and 1997. The reference industry is food.

Table 6. Regressions explaining U.S. manufacturing parents' share in total U.S. manufacturing exports, 1966-97

Variable	(1)	(2)	(3)
Constant	-122.15 **	-136.35 **	-14.19
	(-1.87)	(-2.07)	(-0.71)
USRDSALE U.S. industry R&D as a percentage of current output	-1.20	-1.15	2.41 ***
	(-0.82)	(-0.78)	(4.48)
PMNEINT U.S. parents' foreign employment as a percentage of their total employment	1.24 ***	1.18 ***	1.31 ***
	(3.39)	(3.22)	(6.33)
IMPCOMP Imports as a percentage of apparent consumption in U.S. industry	0.19	0.03	-0.38
	(0.35)	(0.05)	(-1.35)
TECH Computing power per dollar [inverse of log(price/millions of instructions per second)]	-382.11 **		-373.12 **
	(-2.08)		(-2.38)
SCALE Plant scale in U.S. industry [log((employees/establishment)]	19.82 **	18.85 **	7.37 ***
	(2.62)	(2.47)	(4.12)
TIME		-0.40	
		(-1.58)	
Industry dummies			
Chemicals	15.74	16.53	
	(1.45)	(1.50)	
Primary metal	-14.41	-12.15	
	(-0.86)	(-0.72)	
Fabricated metal	14.74	13.85	
	(1.33)	(1.23)	
Machinery	24.22 *	25.21 *	
	(1.90)	(1.93)	
Electrical	8.41	11.71	
	(0.45)	(0.63)	
Motor vehicles and equipment	2.91	8.00	
	(0.13)	(0.35)	
Other transport (mainly aircraft)	38.52 *	38.95 *	
	(1.63)	(1.63)	
Other industry dummies	n/s	n/s	
No. of observations	101	101	101
Adj. R^2	0.68	0.67	0.60
F-stat	11.10 ***	10.78 ***	30.84 ***
Durbin-Watson	2.04	2.04	1.49

n/s not shown but included in the model. ***, **, and * indicate significance at the 1%, 5%, and 10% levels respectively. The dependent variable is PXUSX U.S. parents' total exports as a percentage of total U.S. exports. Observations are from seventeen 2-digit manufacturing industries (excluding tobacco) and six time periods: 1966, 1977, 1982, 1994, 1989, and 1997. The reference industry is food.

Table 7. Regressions explaining intrafirm shares in U.S. manufacturing parents' total exports, 1966-97

Variable	(1)	(2)	(3)
Constant	22.36	14.70	58.78 ***
	(0.78)	(0.50)	(4.23)
PRDSALE U.S. parents' R&D as a percentage of sales	1.94 **	1.83 *	1.78 **
	(2.05)	(1.95)	(2.60)
PMNEINT U.S. parents' foreign employment as a percentage of their total employment	0.37 **	0.36 **	0.72 ***
	(2.07)	(2.02)	(4.68)
PMNEHSP Affiliate-affiliate trade share in U.S. majority-owned foreign affiliates' sales	0.36	0.40	0.77 **
	(1.19)	(1.32)	(2.40)
IMPCOMP Imports as a percentage of apparent consumption in U.S. industry	0.51 **	0.53 **	0.47 **
	(1.91)	(2.02)	(2.03)
TECH Computing power per dollar [inverse of log(price/millions of instructions per second)]	-220.25 **		-370.79 ***
	(-2.49)		(-3.38)
SCALE Plant scale in U.S. industry [log((employees/establishment)^{2})]	-0.19	-0.65	-3.65 ***
	(-0.06)	(-0.20)	(-3.25)
TIME		-0.32 ***	
		(-2.68)	
Industry dummies			
Chemicals	9.24	9.54	
	(1.46)	(1.50)	
Primary metal	-3.85	-3.51	
	(-0.51)	(-0.47)	
Fabricated metal	8.35	7.90	
	(1.59)	(1.52)	
Machinery	13.46 *	12.80 *	
	(1.80)	(1.72)	
Electrical	-1.80	-1.42	
	(-0.21)	(-0.17)	
Motor vehicles and equipment	28.98 ***	29.57 ***	
	(2.69)	(2.80)	
Other transport (mainly aircraft)	-16.31 *	-15.14 *	
	(-1.85)	(-1.73)	
Other industry dummies	n/s	n/s	
No. of observations	102	102	102
Adj. R^2	0.82	0.82	0.51
F-stat	22.05 ***	22.34 ***	18.62 ***
Durbin-Watson	2.13	2.17	0.72

n/s not shown but included in the model. ***, **, and * indicate significance at the 1%, 5%, and 10% levels respectively. The dependent variable is PIFXPX U.S. parents' intrafirm exports as a percentage of U.S. parents' total exports. Observations are from seventeen 2-digit manufacturing industries (excluding tobacco) and six time periods: 1966, 1977, 1982, 1994, 1989, and 1997. The reference industry is food.

Table 8. U.S. exports to U.S. majority-owned foreign affiliates as a percentage of total U.S. manufacturing exports, and percentage of the former that is shipped intrafirm by U.S. parents, 1966-97

Industry	U.S. exports to manufacturing MOFAs as a % of total U.S. manufacturing exports *						U.S. exports received intrafirm from U.S. parents as a % of total U.S. exports received by U.S. MOFAs **					
	1966	*1977*	*1982*	*1989*	*1994*	*1997*	*1966*	*1977*	*1982*	*1989*	*1994*	*1997*
Manufacturing	24.1	26.9	21.5	23.3	23.0	22.6	82.6	81.6	83.1	86.8	83.3	84.5
Food and kindred products	10.3	13.4	16.8	13.7	10.5	9.1	53.1	46.6	50.8	70.5	80.1	77.2
Chemicals and allied products	27.2	28.2	20.2	20.5	22.2	24.3	84.5	88.3	81.7	88.5	84.7	90.7
Primary metals products	7.4	11.2	6.0	6.2	4.0	3.3	97.3	84.9	64.7	83.4	73.5	71.2
Fabricated metal products	26.1	11.5	8.0	11.0	12.2	10.2	71.0	68.7	83.6	77.9	67.0	77.5
Industrial machinery and equipment	15.9	14.2	12.4	21.0	17.9	17.3	98.5	92.6	94.4	92.8	88.6	88.7
Electronic and other electric equipment	25.6	26.3	25.5	24.8	23.8	23.8	72.1	85.8	89.5	89.7	94.6	92.1
Motor vehicles and equipment	56.6	89.8	87.1	99.1	85.4	89.8	112.2	80.7	81.4	86.1	78.9	79.1
Other transport (including aircraft)	48.0	2.6	2.3	1.4	3.1	2.8	20.1	48.7	50.8	49.2	34.8	32.5
Tobacco products	82.4	32.3	n/a	5.0	2.0	10.0	17.2	n/a	86.7	68.0	76.4	100.0
Textile products and apparel	6.2	13.1	14.8	8.1	4.5	3.6	53.9	63.6	86.7	73.8	73.6	76.7
Lumber, wood, furniture, and fixtures	3.4	2.6	1.8	3.2	5.7	4.9	75.1	n/a	78.7	82.1	58.9	83.2
Paper and allied products	32.1	23.8	14.3	13.0	16.4	13.5	57.5	60.9	72.0	63.9	77.5	84.0
Printing and publishing	15.1	9.5	5.3	4.1	7.1	6.8	60.7	89.2	88.9	87.9	79.2	96.0
Rubber products	111.5	45.1	34.8	29.1	26.8	25.8	117.5	81.6	77.1	85.4	85.0	81.3
Miscellaneous plastics products	21.3	8.6	19.2	20.0	17.5	14.1	116.2	80.6	79.1	87.6	91.2	86.5
Glass products	16.8	16.1	13.0	24.4	4.7	18.2	106.7	80.9	88.5	82.6	61.7	73.1
Stone, clay, and nonmetallic mineral pr	25.4	24.2	19.6	20.1	18.1	16.5	95.0	71.9	79.0	75.0	81.9	87.4
Instruments and related products	31.7	24.4	22.8	20.7	17.0	16.4	80.3	94.9	97.4	90.0	92.9	92.6

Source: U.S. export figures are from U.S. Department of Commerce, Statistical Abstract of the United States, various issues; multinational export figures are from U.S. Department of Commerce, U.S. Direct Investment Abroad, various issues.

*The U.S. Commerce Department classifies multinational export data by industry of U.S. parent and U.S. export figures by product. This, in some cases, leads to estimates of intrafirm shares that are greater than 100 percent of the total.

**Author's estimates, in some cases, lead to shares that are greater than 100 percent.

n/a not available; figures in italics are author's estimates.

www.ingramcontent.com/pod-product-compliance
Lightning Source LLC
Chambersburg PA
CBHW080924290526
45795CB00007BA/2647